Work 2.0: How Artificial Intelligence is Changing the Future of Work

CEO's Advice on Computer Science

Warren H. Lau

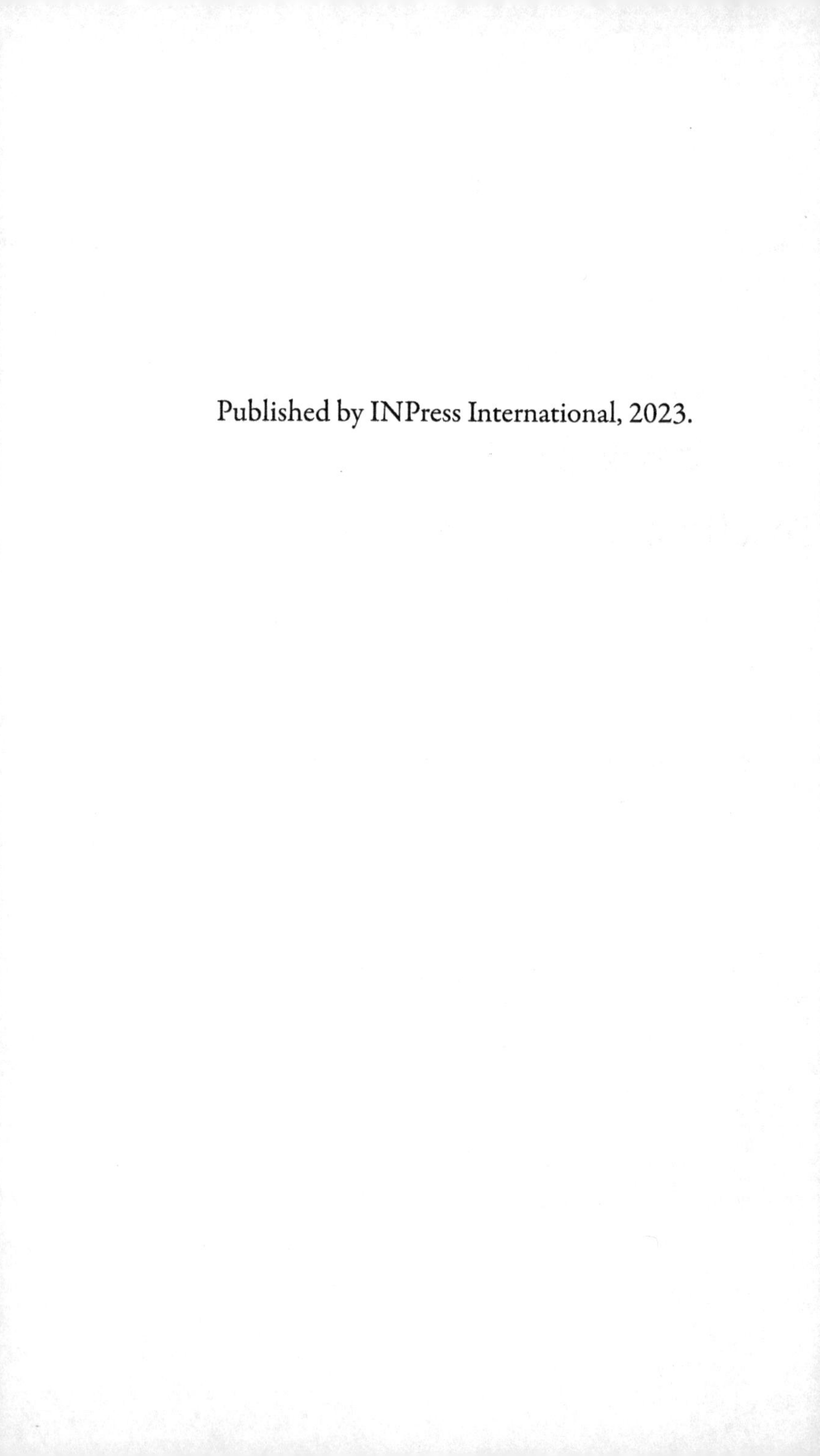

Published by INPress International, 2023.

WORK 2.0: HOW ARTIFICIAL INTELLIGENCE IS CHANGING THE FUTURE OF WORK

First edition. April 22, 2023.

Copyright © 2023 Warren H. Lau.

ISBN: 979-8223279426

Written by Warren H. Lau.

Table of Contents

To My Beloved Family

WORK 2.0: How Artificial Intelligence is Changing the Future of Work

Preface

The labor market is undergoing rapid change as a result of AI and automation. In this book, we investigate what simulated intelligence is meaning for various businesses and callings, and deal pragmatic guidance on the most proficient method to explore this new scene. Whether you're a new student searching for your first job, or an old pro trying to remain important in your field, this book will assist you with understanding how artificial intelligence is changing the world of work, and how you can use this innovation to advance your career.

Introduction: The AI Revolution and Its Impact on Work

In a world where AI has replaced most jobs, we would see a significant shift in the way work is done. Augmenting human capabilities with technology would become the norm, with machines performing tasks that were once exclusive to humans. Jobs almost jobs would be replaced with AI capabilities performing functions like humans, making it easier for companies to streamline their operations and reduce costs. However, even though people may lose their jobs, they will adapt by finding new ways to complement work done by machines.

Imagine a world where AI has replaced most jobs. The workforce would be dominated by intelligent machines, and people would have to adapt to this new reality. Governments might consider subsidizing job replacement or boosting the minimum wage to help those who lose their jobs. However, even though some people may lose their jobs, they will adapt by finding new ways to complement work done by machines.

Imagine a world where AI has replaced most jobs. This world would be characterized by a significant technological advancement that has created many more jobs in tech and other professionals. The use of AI to add artificial intelligence and automate industries would replace many jobs, but it would also grow high wage jobs such as those in insights robotics. This new working environment would require new skills that people can acquire through retraining or education to remain relevant in the job market. As certain employments are replaced, new types of employment would appear, accompanied by lower wage structures as machines assist IoT. However, even though some people may lose their jobs, they will adapt by finding new ways to complement work done by machines.

Imagine a world where AI has replaced most jobs through the automated existing tasks and partial automation. Jobs so called adjacencies will emerge, wherein technologies that require other tasks will be created. Tasks jobs that were once handled by humans are now done by machines. The new jobs to be created will require human participation in terms of participation supervision, cooperating people with machines to complete remaining jobs and activities.

Imagine a world where AI has replaced most jobs. This world would be characterized by dynamism rising productivity growth, as machines would be able to carry out tasks much faster and more efficiently. While many people may lose their jobs due to automation, there would also be many new opportunities for those who are willing to learn new skills and adapt to the changing job market. The economy would continue to experience additional economic growth as many jobs that were previously done by humans are now taken over by machines.

Imagine a world where AI has replaced most jobs. The automation would displace many workers, and the number of automated jobs could reach 800 million by 2030. However, this trend could create 97 million new jobs in other categories. Machines would have replaced 85 million jobs, but the economy would continue to experience additional economic growth as many jobs that were previously done by humans are now taken over by machines. According to many experts, artificial intelligence will switch job categories and create new professions. The McKinsey Global Institute reckons that machines will replace approximately one-fifth of existing occupations.

Artificial intelligence (AI) has the potential to revolutionize many sectors of our society. Developed AI systems can perform complex tasks and learn from experience, leading to significant implications for how we live and work. Machines programs can take over many people's jobs, which will have a profound impact on our economy and society. The McKinsey Global Institute reckons that machines will replace approximately one-fifth of existing occupations. This means that robots could achieve technology that can replace humans in industries like manufacturing, transportation, customer service, and even healthcare. However, this also means that AI systems are benefitting many people by taking over tedious jobs or those with high-risk factors. The way AI is developed needs to be closely monitored by management university and applied sciences to ensure that it benefits society as a whole rather than just a select few.

Imagine a world where AI has replaced most jobs. This would mean that machines and algorithms would be doing humans jobs, and people would have to adapt to a new way of life. The world would look very different, with AI technology becoming the norm in every industry. Businesses would put AI technology to work, optimizing many different processes and meeting their needs. Emerging technologies would make it possible for businesses to have safer processes that are more efficient than ever before. If you want to grow your business or your company, you need to create new opportunities by putting many humans out of work and replacing them with AI technology.

If we were to imagine a world where AI has replaced most jobs, it is easy to envision a future where artificial intelligence has eliminated many current jobs that require repetitive and time-consuming tasks. With AI taking on these roles, people would be left with more time to achieve greater things, such as pursuing their passions or developing new skills. However, this new future would require significant changes in the education infrastructure to support people in acquiring new skills and adapting to the changing work environment. The good reason for this shift is that AI can take care of the mundane tasks, while humans can focus on more creative and complex projects. It is estimated that up to 99% of jobs could be eliminated by AI, but this does not mean that humans will become redundant. Instead, humans can become strategic employees who manage and maintain these technologies for optimal performance.

If AI were to replace most jobs, the world would see catastrophic job losses and a significant shift in the job market. The replacement of jobs by AI would eliminate many blue-collar workers needed for tasks such as driving and supermarkets stacking shelves. In the short term, there may not be enough evidence to suggest that AI will create more jobs than it eliminates. However, in the future, it is a good predictor that AI will offer other possibilities for workers.

Imagine a world where AI has replaced most jobs. The industries of nanotechnology and synthetic biology, for example, would require human judgment and certain skill sets that AI cannot replicate. Robot manufacturers would change job descriptions to employ many people in new industries that AI cannot do. However, AI could kill jobs that involve repetitive roles or calculable tasks. This could help create better ones for humans who can focus on more complex roles that require creativity and decision-making skills.

Introduction to CEO's Advice on Computer Science

Let's face it. The traditional schooling system's focus on computer sci ence is severely inadequate. In order to survive an ever developing com puter driven world, in order to equip yourselves or your children with sufficient computer knowledge, so to have better employment or better living standards, the smart choice will be to seek new solutions from ex perts who have already spent decades in this field.

And that is why the cyber education series, "CEO's Advice on Computer Science", is published for you.

In this series, the most sought after topics in Computer Science will be covered, including SEO, ASO, Cybersecurity, Computer Programming, Coding Skills, eCommerce, and other useful techniques that you would find very useful in your future career path, whether you wish to seek a job in large companies or tech firms, or even though you wish to run your own startup.

The Rise of AI in Different Industries

What is artificial intelligence?

Artificial intelligence (AI) is a computer system that can mimic the way human intelligence operates. It usually consists of two main components: algorithms and data. Algorithms are a series of algorithms that enable computers to complete specific tasks and make decisions based on given data. Data is the data collected by a computer from the required information. The development of artificial intelligence technology began in the 1950s. The first artificial intelligence application is logic based speech recognition, which can convert speech into text without human intervention. The second application is rule-based rule matching, which is an automated mechanism that can complete tasks without human intervention. In recent years, deep learning technology has made significant progress and has been widely applied in image and speech recognition.

In today's profession, artificial intelligence (AI) has numerous industry-specific applications and has emerged as an indispensable tool. Businesses can personalize customer experiences and boost sales by utilizing AI to assist machine learning algorithms. AI is also being used by sales technology to improve sales HR operations. Fabricating promoting is profiting from this innovation by enhancing tasks producing and responding to questions logical analyses. In addition, healthcare sales are incorporating AI into the healthcare industry to enhance life quality.

Artificial intelligence is being utilized in different callings, including medical services and deals, to upgrade efficiency and navigation. AI uses data to make better decisions and predict what will happen in the future. Machines are taking choices, which saves time and increments exactness in handling billions of information in practically no time. Nonetheless, integrating cyberattacks into man-made intelligence frameworks represents a huge test as they can prompt troublesome cyberattacks that might hurt organizations. Then again, artificial intelligence is working with different innovations to make organizations more proficient via computerizing redundant assignments.

In contrast, AI is collaborating with other technologies to automate routine tasks and increase business efficiency. Numerous technological advancements and the use of lead artificial intelligence have transformed a variety of professions. Specialization has become more important in today's job market, which has led to advancement in positions that require particular skills like creativity and problem-solving. However, it also indicates that there is a chance that some jobs will be automated. Blue-collar jobs that require quantitative problem-solving skills show the dramatic impact of automation.

The use of AI systems will have a wide range of effects on our current field. The term "artificial intelligence" has been around for decades and has developed into the sophisticated AI systems we see today, despite being frequently depicted as a futuristic technology. From our most loved science fiction motion pictures to quantum processing, artificial intelligence is altering numerous areas. As we keep on growing genuine man-made intelligence, it will assume a significant part in causing reality to look like what was once considered unimaginable. However, using this technology for work presents some difficulties. The apprehension made by science fiction films where simulated intelligence frameworks make individuals old isn't totally unwarranted. Although these systems may not take over the world as depicted in the movies, they do have the potential to perform certain tasks in place of human workers.

Artificial Intelligence is being executed in different businesses, including finance, to build productivity and precision. Automated chatbots and the application of machine learning, which enables learning adaptive intelligence, are commonly referred to as AI. AI is utilized in cognitive computing and algorithm trading in the financial sector. Although these systems may not take over the world as depicted in the movies, they do have the potential to perform certain tasks in place of human workers. Nonetheless, this innovation likewise accompanies difficulties, for example, moral worries encompassing the utilization of machines that can supplant human knowledge. Regardless of these difficulties, exchanging mechanization and other simulated intelligence based advances supplement work by performing assignments that require high proficiency and precision.

The use of artificial intelligence can liberate humans from repetitive and non creative work. Artificial intelligence has brought huge benefits to many industries, including manufacturing, healthcare, retail, transportation, and manufacturing. These technologies will enable workers to better serve customers and reduce costs by eliminating certain tasks. Artificial intelligence can also reduce the burden on employers and make it easier to expand into new markets. Artificial intelligence may make each of us worried about our future: what impact will automation have on workers in your field in the coming years? What role will artificial intelligence play in our workplace? If we don't understand our work, how can we ensure that it won't be replaced by automation in the coming years? If you are looking for a skill in your career that sets you apart, artificial intelligence may help you find these skills. Artificial intelligence can provide you with more opportunities to stand out in the job market. Artificial intelligence technology has been widely applied in many fields, including healthcare, manufacturing, retail, and transportation. However, some people may argue that artificial intelligence technology may replace some job positions. Nevertheless, this does not mean that these job positions will disappear. In this article, we will explore the benefits and challenges of artificial intelligence for workers and employers in some of the most popular industries. We will also explore how artificial intelligence technology can help people better serve their customers.

Artificial intelligence has become an important technology in many industries, such as industrial robots replacing human workers in factories, and smartphone applications allowing customers to purchase products online. Artificial intelligence has greatly improved manufacturers' operations and product quality. Some large companies have started using artificial intelligence to improve customer service quality and improve the operation of the entire enterprise. Artificial intelligence can also help companies reduce costs, for example, by utilizing machine learning algorithms, companies can more accurately predict equipment failures, thereby reducing costs. This enables employees in many industries to earn higher income by gaining more value from their work.

Artificial intelligence can improve work efficiency and save employers time and costs. For example, artificial intelligence can reduce errors in order processing and inventory management. By eliminating repetitive tasks, enterprises can reduce operational costs. Artificial intelligence can also make it easier for employees to adapt to new environments. For example, in the retail industry, artificial intelligence can make it easier for customers to find the products they want and keep inventory where they need it most. By using artificial intelligence technology, enterprises can reduce operational costs, improve employee work efficiency and customer satisfaction, thereby bringing higher profits to the enterprise.

With the help of artificial intelligence, some jobs may disappear, such as manufacturing, retail, transportation, etc. However, some tasks still require human participation. For example, in the manufacturing industry, the use of robots and automated machines can help workers complete repetitive and monotonous tasks. In addition, artificial intelligence can also reduce costs by eliminating certain tasks. Therefore, although artificial intelligence may replace certain job positions, there is still a lot of work that humans need to complete. In addition, in the coming years, some employers may be negatively affected by artificial intelligence. For example, people may lose their jobs or take on more responsibilities within the company. However, these are all temporary, and with the continuous development and progress of technology, people's dependence on artificial intelligence will gradually decrease. With the passage of time and the accumulation of experience, we can see that artificial intelligence will work together with humans and take on more responsibilities.

Artificial intelligence (AI) is a branch of computer science aimed at enabling machines to perform tasks that humans can complete, rather than replacing humans. This technology is called artificial intelligence and is often described as the ability to simulate human intelligence through computers. In the past few decades, artificial intelligence has developed to an incredible level. In the coming decades, it may become much more powerful than any technology you are currently using. With the widespread application of artificial intelligence technology in various industries, how can we utilize it to help us cope with many potential challenges that may arise in the future? Before we discuss the impact of AI on everyone, let's take a look at how it helps businesses and governments respond to challenges. This will be a good start. In this process, we will use artificial intelligence technology to provide real-time insights and insights to help us better understand what is happening. This means using AI to improve efficiency and productivity. For example, by analyzing a large amount of data and machine learning models to determine which regions are most likely to experience earthquakes, to help prepare in advance and reduce property damage. With the continuous development of artificial intelligence technology, many industries will use it to meet specific needs and provide a better customer experience. In this process, we will see how artificial intelligence technology has penetrated into many industries and job positions.

The application of artificial intelligence can help governments and businesses reduce expenses, improve efficiency, and provide a better customer experience. They then worked with the United States Geological Survey to develop emergency plans for areas with the greatest potential earthquake impact. By applying artificial intelligence to these fields, we can use fewer resources to improve efficiency and reduce property damage.

WORK 2.0: HOW ARTIFICIAL INTELLIGENCE IS CHANGING THE FUTURE OF WORK

This is a very important example for governments and businesses. For example, using artificial intelligence technology to identify market trends, customer feedback, and predict potential customer churn and retention issues. This helps businesses better understand consumer behavior and needs, and take corresponding measures to optimize customer experience.

Artificial intelligence technology is a hot topic for banks and financial institutions. It provides financial services by installing applications on our phones. With it, you can easily apply for loans, investments, or deposits. Using artificial intelligence technology, we can process a large amount of data and use machine learning to quickly and accurately recognize patterns. For example, a banking application driven by artificial intelligence can help you apply for credit cards and loans. It can be reviewed within a few days after you submit your application, so you don't have to queue up at the bank anymore. Through artificial intelligence technology, we can also input our personal information into blockchain based networks to ensure that we do not leak any personal information. This will provide us with safer and more accurate information. As more and more people use artificial intelligence technology, we will see more banks and financial institutions adopting AI technology.

Artificial intelligence can also be used in the healthcare industry. For example, you can use it to predict the health status of patients and make corresponding treatment plans. Artificial intelligence can improve the efficiency and accuracy of doctors by predicting and processing large amounts of data. For example, artificial intelligence can be used to classify and classify patients based on their medical history, symptoms, signs, and other medical information upon admission. In addition, artificial intelligence can also help doctors diagnose and treat patients faster. If one of these factors is proven to be accurate, doctors will be able to take early measures to prevent cancer, which can provide treatment for patients before undergoing surgery. This not only helps to treat cancer better, but also reduces treatment costs, making healthcare cheaper and easier to access.

In most cases, data analysis is the most widely used field of artificial intelligence (AI). However, some more subtle areas, such as customer relationship management and marketing, can also utilize artificial intelligence. When analyzing a large amount of data, machine learning can be used to predict the next trend. Machine learning is a form of artificial intelligence. This technology uses algorithms to learn patterns from data. Then, the algorithm uses these patterns to predict future behavior. Machine learning can also use data to learn new datasets and rules, thereby providing more accurate prediction results. This method also helps to interpret historical data to help businesses understand their behavior. In addition to learning patterns from historical data, machine learning can also detect and avoid human errors. For example, by using a large amount of data for training and testing, machine learning can learn how to avoid manual errors and improve accuracy.

In the customer service industry, artificial intelligence technology can help enterprises better manage customer data. According to a study by artificial intelligence and machine learning research company Autonomy, customer service using artificial intelligence can reduce complaints by over 30%. This means that companies using artificial intelligence technology for customer service can handle problems more effectively. Artificial intelligence can analyze a large amount of data, such as customer comments and complaints, and classify and interpret them. In this way, enterprises can make decisions based on the analysis results. For example, a company using artificial intelligence technology can determine customers' preferences by analyzing their messages posted on social media. By doing so, they can obtain more comprehensive data on customer preferences and trends in a short period of time. This will help businesses better understand customers and provide better services and products based on their preferences.

Business process automation is one of the most widely used areas in artificial intelligence technology. Business process automation refers to the process of automating an enterprise's business processes to improve efficiency, save time, and improve accuracy. Business process automation can perform many tasks as needed, such as identifying data, automatic processing, monitoring, and reporting data. In the field of healthcare, artificial intelligence technology can be used to identify and optimize patient data. For example, artificial intelligence can be used to identify specific diseases and automatically transmit this information to doctors or nurses. This will help diagnose patients faster and improve treatment outcomes. In the manufacturing industry, artificial intelligence technology can be used to improve product design and development. For example, manufacturing companies can use artificial intelligence technology to design and test new products, and verify their accuracy and efficiency in a short period of time. This will greatly shorten the product's time to market and reduce production costs. In addition, artificial intelligence technology can be used for real-time monitoring of product quality in the supply chain. This information can help manufacturers better understand the quality of their products and adjust production plans in a timely manner.

Artificial intelligence can be utilized in numerous ways in the manufacturing sector. Additionally, it has the potential to assist businesses in enhancing efficiency and lowering energy and waste consumption. Artificial intelligence can also be used to find flaws in products and take the appropriate actions based on those flaws. For instance, businesses can enhance their manufacturing processes and better anticipate customer requirements by analyzing products using artificial intelligence. The manufacturing sector typically makes use of artificial intelligence in the following ways: upgrading item plan: utilizing man-made consciousness to enhance item plan to lessen costs and work on quality. Preventative upkeep: Downtime can be reduced, costs can be reduced, and efficiency can be improved by implementing preventive maintenance strategies and predicting the state of equipment using machine learning and artificial intelligence. Machine helped analysis: Accuracy can be enhanced and downtime reduced by utilizing machine learning to assist in identifying faults and potential issues. Naturally, artificial intelligence can be utilized in other fields as well. For instance, by coordinating man-made consciousness innovation with the Web of Things (IoT) into plants, ventures can more readily comprehend the presentation and proficiency of their creation processes.

Artificial intelligence (AI) will bring new opportunities and challenges to work in many fields. According to Olivier Riccardo in his article "Olivier Riccardo: The Benefits and Challenges of Artificial Intelligence for Workers in Different Industries," AI will have an impact in several areas: manufacturing: AI can be used to replace workers in certain jobs. In the manufacturing industry, automation has been proven to be a powerful tool for improving productivity and has been well utilized in the past decade. To achieve this, machines must operate more efficiently and be able to perform tasks faster. However, these changes may affect some workers, especially those who lack skilled skills or abilities. Healthcare: Artificial intelligence can be used to assist doctors in diagnosing diseases. Although AI technology has been proven to reduce the workload of doctors and improve diagnostic efficiency, there are still some technical obstacles to AI. For example, AI may replace specific medical laboratory work. For those without a medical background, this may be a challenge. Agriculture: Agriculture is using many robots for production. For example, drones can work in many fields and liberate humans from manual labor. Due to AI's ability to create more accurate reports, agricultural workers may have more time to engage in higher-level work. For example, there are many automated robots in power plants that can replace workers in easier, safer, and more reliable jobs.

Manufacturing is an important field of AI application. Although AI technology has been proven to improve productivity and productivity, its applications are still limited. In the manufacturing industry, automated machines can make workers' tasks easier and safer to complete. However, if machines cannot operate within their capabilities, manual operation is required. AI technology can solve these problems, but they cannot completely replace workers.

The AI in the healthcare field is constantly developing, which is good news for many people. AI can help doctors diagnose diseases and reduce their workload, while also improving patient care to provide better treatment. However, there are still some technical barriers to the application of AI in the healthcare field, such as a lack of training: many people do not have a medical background, which makes it difficult for them to use AI to diagnose diseases. Data privacy: Most healthcare systems rely on data. Therefore, if data is stored in an unauthorized organization, it may cause problems.

AI brings enormous opportunities to agriculture. Automation and drones can greatly improve productivity, which means farmers can reduce working hours and free themselves from heavy physical labor. AI can more accurately monitor crop conditions and help better plan yields and prices. In addition, AI can also reduce the content of pesticides and insecticides in agricultural products. However, agricultural workers will face some challenges. Although AI can improve productivity and reduce worker demand, farmers still have to use a large amount of labor to complete their work. This means they must work harder and possess the necessary skills to survive in agriculture. Furthermore, although AI can assist farmers in better planning and management, it will not completely replace human labor.

Although AI can bring benefits in many fields, there are also some issues that need to be addressed. For example, artificial intelligence can be used to assist doctors in diagnosing diseases, but this may not necessarily improve doctors' work efficiency. In addition, medical institutions in certain regions may not be willing to allow patients to use artificial intelligence. In the field of agriculture, robots are helping farmers produce more crops. Due to the potential of artificial intelligence to improve farmers' productivity, these robots will become helpers for farmers. Due to AI's ability to increase crop yields and reduce waste, robots can help farmers achieve higher yields during the harvest season.

The application of artificial intelligence in the retail industry can reduce labor and have an impact on workers and employers. These benefits include: - reducing workload, thereby increasing the number of employees, thereby improving productivity and reducing costs- Improving customer loyalty by providing a better customer experience- Increase employee health and welfare, and save costs by eliminating duplicate labor- Improve security as it reduces the number of people entering and leaving the store. Although artificial intelligence applications in the retail industry have made significant progress, their true advantages have not yet been fully utilized. As artificial intelligence continues to become more mature, we can expect to see more applications of artificial intelligence emerge. Especially in the retail industry, artificial intelligence will change the entire industry.

AI will help the construction industry become smarter because it will make construction workers safer. By reducing the factors that may cause injury and illness during the construction process, the incidence of accidents can be reduced. For example, artificial intelligence systems can help workers avoid falling from heights or coming into contact with toxic materials, both of which can lead to injury or even death. On the construction site, if workers are not careful, AI will monitor the risk factors and automatically respond. This will improve the safety level and efficiency of workers, as they do not need to personally inspect risk factors. In addition, AI can also reduce the labor demand in the construction industry. Research shows that before using AI, the annual labor demand in the United States was 7 million people.

AI has important applications in many industries, for example, in the retail industry, artificial intelligence can improve customer experience and reduce costs. In other industries, AI is also used to improve productivity and reduce risks. For example, in the logistics industry, artificial intelligence can assist in handling transportation problems, rather than being manually completed by humans. AI can also enhance employees' safety awareness and safety, rather than engaging workers in dangerous tasks. Some companies may be concerned that using AI may lead to job losses, but AI technology will continue to create new jobs. As AI technology becomes increasingly complex and automated, it needs to be regulated and regulated. However, some people believe that this change will not affect the wages of existing workers, as AI has important applications in most industries.

Preparing for an AI-Driven Future

Over the past few decades, artificial intelligence (AI) has been a hot topic in the technology sector. We now live in a world driven by AI, and AI has altered work, education, and lifestyle. The era of artificial intelligence will see collaboration between humans and machines. This possibility will excite a lot of people, but not everyone is sure how it will affect them. Because some jobs are more likely to be affected by artificial intelligence than others, many people fear losing their jobs. In this article, we will examine the effect of computerized reasoning on professions and how individuals can help themselves and their kids to adapt to the appearance of the man-made brainpower period. In addition, we will look at skills and ideas for becoming better workers in the 21st century. For more data, kindly allude to the accompanying article.

Why is it necessary to master artificial intelligence skills?

If you want to become a better worker in the 21st century, then you must understand how artificial intelligence affects your career. If you feel uneasy about the future or want to do something for your future, learning artificial intelligence skills is a good starting point. With the advancement of AI technology, many people may worry that their skills will be eliminated in the future. Mastering artificial intelligence skills not only provides you with a way to leverage the benefits of AI, but also makes you more competitive in the job market. For example, if you want to become a teacher, you must learn how to use AI to organize courses more effectively and enable students to achieve the best results in the classroom. If you want to become a salesperson, understanding how to use AI to optimize customer service will help you establish your own brand and improve sales performance.

What are the best job skills for the 21st century?

For those who want to succeed in the era of artificial intelligence, the following are some skills worth learning: - Learning and adaptability: Over time, AI will dominate the workplace. In order to maintain competitiveness and position, it is necessary to master new skills and learn new knowledge. To maintain a leading position, it is necessary to have the ability to learn and adapt- Self motivation and self-management skills: AI enables employees to work anywhere and be largely independent of their employers. To maintain competitiveness in this constantly changing world, it is necessary to possess self-motivation and self-management abilities- Leadership and leadership skills: AI will change the role and role of leaders. In order to adapt to the future work environment, leaders must possess leadership skills and collaborate with others. In order to meet the constantly changing needs of an organization, leaders must possess the ability to manage and motivate themselves.

How to prepare yourself and your children?

Although the emergence of artificial intelligence may cause many people to lose their jobs, there are also some professions that can benefit from it. There are many suggestions and suggestions that can help people adapt to new technologies. A good start is to learn some knowledge about artificial intelligence. For example, the development of artificial intelligence and machine learning is very rapid. Machine learning and artificial intelligence have become topics of interest to many people. If you are interested in artificial intelligence, it

WORK 2.0: HOW ARTIFICIAL INTELLIGENCE IS CHANGING THE FUTURE OF WORK

is important to learn more about it, so that you can understand how to use machine learning to help you complete your tasks. Here, we have some suggestions for your reference.

Artificial intelligence (AI) is becoming a topic of increasing concern and will also affect various industries. Former US President Obama once said, "In the next 30 years, we will compete with machines for jobs." Of course, in the future world, no one will engage in heavy physical labor to support their families, but will be replaced by various new technologies such as artificial intelligence and automation. These new technologies will completely change the way we work, and this change has already begun to emerge. If we want to achieve success in the future, we must learn to use artificial intelligence technology to improve efficiency. But the skills and knowledge required for AI are very different from before. In order to help people better master the skills and knowledge required for AI, we have prepared a list of AI skills for everyone, so that they can find the right career direction.

1. Data scientist

Data scientists are a profession that uses data. They are experts in big data processing and analysis, able to collect, clean up, and organize data, and transform it into meaningful information so that enterprises can make wise decisions. Data scientists need to master various skills, including programming, statistics, mathematics, and statistics. They usually use programming languages such as Python to process and analyze data. For anyone who wants to learn or engage in big data work, learning a statistical analysis technology is very important. Statistical analysis techniques can help you discover patterns, identify problems, and draw conclusions from a large amount of data.

2. Algorithm Engineer

Algorithm engineers are professionals in the field of AI, proficient in mathematics and statistical knowledge, capable of designing and implementing machine learning algorithms, and using them to solve problems. Due to the challenging nature of AI, it requires a significant amount of professional knowledge. Although machine learning and deep learning models can help us solve problems, these models typically require a large amount of data to be implemented. Without professional algorithm engineers, we will not be able to extract useful information from massive amounts of data. That's why if you want to find a job in the AI field, you need to master this knowledge. Having deep mathematical and statistical skills can help you find a job that suits you. In addition, you also need to be proficient in machine learning and deep learning, able to clean, structure, and denoise data, and then solve problems through model training and optimization.

3. Machine Learning Engineer

Machine learning engineers are one of the most scarce positions in the AI field, and this position requires very high skills from engineers. Machine learning engineers need to be proficient in various programming languages and be very familiar with the basic knowledge of machine learning. They also need to be able to solve common data problems, including classification, regression, and clustering. In addition, machine learning engineers must also have strong programming skills and be able to write algorithms for different tasks. They also need to understand some important statistical concepts, such as least squares, decision trees, and Bayesian theorem. Machine learning engineers are usually indispensable members of a team, working closely with AI managers and other team members. Their job responsibilities include developing plans, selecting datasets, creating algorithm models, evaluating results, writing code, and communicating with other engineers.

4. Graphic artist

AI can accomplish many tasks, but an important part of it is creating graphics. This is different from humans, who can express their thoughts through painting, carving, and creation. AI, on the other hand, can only program and design through programs, so they do not have their own creativity. If you want to become an excellent graphic artist, you need to master some basic painting skills and be proficient in using software such as Photoshop and Illustrator to draw images. If you have a talent for painting, you can also generate interesting images through machine learning.

I have found that turning into a certified information researcher as a novice in the field is troublesome. I will discuss some of the best resources on information science in this article, which will help you acquire the necessary skills to become a researcher. What capacities must we secure? If you want to work as a data scientist, you need to know what data science is and how to use it. This article will cover all of the most fundamental aspects of data science, machine learning, algorithm engineering, and graphic design.

1. What is Data Science

Data Science is a new field that uses data, information science, and numerical methods to solve real-world problems. We use AI calculations in this field to break down, investigate, and imagine information. Measurable strategies and models are normal names for these calculations. This extremely broad field encompasses transportation, finance, healthcare, commerce, and other related fields. A wide range of subjects are covered by the broad field of data science, including: Statistics: Science of Data: Using Machine Learning to Process and Examine Data for Useful Insights Finding Answers for Information Issues in Organizations and Businesses Calculation Designing: Creating algorithms that are capable of efficiently processing large amounts of data and producing useful results Using algorithms to discover models, training patterns, and predictions

2. What is machine learning and algorithm engineering

A PC calculation that gains designs from information is known as AI. Algorithms can perform many functions, including classification, regression, clustering, prediction, and others. If you want to work as a data scientist, you need to know the basics of machine learning. The process of creating algorithms that can use mathematical tools to solve problems in the real world is known as algorithm engineering. You will figure out how to advance calculations and apply calculations to true issues in calculation designing. Ensuing to understanding these central data, we can start sorting out some way to apply man-made intelligence to practice. We still need to learn how to use these tools to solve real-world problems, despite our basic comprehension of these ideas.

3. What resources can help you become a data scientist

Once you know everything there is to know about data science, you can start using these resources. If you want to work in the field, the following websites and tools can help you become a data scientist. Kaggle is a website for data science understanding, which gives a huge number of online courses and self-learning materials. Evernote is a free note-taking app that lets you save your favorite content to the cloud and provides note templates. GitHub is a free open-source code library that provides project-building tools and a variety of code libraries. Codecademy, a free online course and learning platform, offers numerous fundamental data science courses and hands-on activities.

Finding Your Career Path in an AI World

There is a saying: The job you are engaged in may be the best job you can do.In the world driven by artificial intelligence, you may ask yourself this question: How would you choose the job that you can do the best? When you decide to pursue a certain job, you must determine what factors drive it and whether they make the job better or make you smarter in the field. This is the key to deciding what you should choose to do. There are three important factors for this: skills, abilities, and motivation. Skills refer to the basic knowledge, skills, and abilities required in this job. For example, language proficiency, writing ability, financial ability, etc. Ability refers to your level of understanding, depth, and breadth of understanding of the job. For example, communication skills, information collection and analysis abilities, etc. Motivation refers to the degree and motivation to which this job can help you do better, which is the degree to which you enjoy the job. There is a saying: Interest is the best teacher. When a person is interested in a certain job, they will invest more time and energy and do it better. When he is not interested in a certain job, he will be perfunctory, and perfunctory will prevent him from realizing his potential and achieving his best. So when considering what profession to pursue, what factors should we consider? Mainly including the following points:

Understand what you want to do and cultivate these abilities in your work

What would you do? Here, I think you may think of many things. For example, you may come up with a project and entrust it to an experienced person. Alternatively, you may want to start a company and have someone else manage it. These things are all very good! But what I want to say is, the best career path is to be clear about what you want to do! After you have figured out what you want to do, you can go find a job that matches it. For example, you have a goal: to become a writer. So this means you need a platform or venue that can create and publish works. When you consider which website to go to, you are thinking about this question: What should I put on my website? So at this point, you can consider where to go and who to find to do these jobs. For example, if you enjoy writing or have strong writing skills, you can consider publishing articles on a blog. If you enjoy working in areas such as business writing, creative writing, and some word games, you can consider writing a blog. For example, if you are good at communicating with people and have strong communication skills, you can consider working as a salesperson or sales consultant. This is the process of clarifying what you want to do. With these ideas in mind, we can now search for a job that suits us. Some people may want to work in some large companies or enterprises; Some people may want to work in some startup companies; Some people may want to work for some freelancers. For these different ideas and practices, we can compare them together. For example, if you want to become a freelancer, then this is one of the best choices. Because many freelancers need to communicate with others to gain inspiration and ideas. When you are not in the company, you can also freely arrange your time, hobbies, lifestyle, etc; When you are in the company, you can achieve growth and progress by reporting to your team or boss. Therefore, once we have determined what we want to do, we can cultivate these abilities by understanding our work. For example, if I want to become a writer or professional writer, I can go to the writing platform to publish articles and earn royalties; If I want to become a sales consultant, I can gain sales inspiration and ideas by communicating and communicating with others; If I want to become a freelancer, I can gain inspiration and ideas through writing and communicating with others. In short, in this process, we must constantly cultivate these abilities! If you are unsure of what you want to do, why not explore more about the jobs or professions in your field of interest? Cultivate the necessary abilities through research and learning in these jobs or professions.

Start with the profession you are interested in

Nowadays, most people graduate from ordinary universities, and some even enter the workplace when they are in high school. These people may not have any interests or ideals in school, which leads to a significant gap between their job positions and their interests and ideals after graduation. In addition, they lack the corresponding professional skills, which leads to repeated setbacks in job hunting. Some people may not find a job after graduating from college and be forced to do jobs they don't like. If we don't know what profession we like, we can choose from the following aspects: (1) Assess our skills and abilities. (2) Assess your interest in other areas. (3) Evaluate the job or profession you are interested in doing. When conducting an evaluation, it is important to pay attention to the following points: (1) Are you interested in other aspects? (2) Do you have the ability to do it? (3) Do you have sufficient knowledge of your interests?

Career planning is a long-term and complex project

If we have a clear career plan for the future and want to know what we want to do in the future, then in daily life, we will have a clearer understanding of our goals and better achieve them. We need to understand that in the process of career development, we will encounter various problems, which is also very normal. However, we need to have a clear understanding of ourselves and know what we will do in the future. If you are not clear about what you want to do, it is easy to get lost in your future life. Moreover, we need to constantly summarize and learn in both work and life. Only by continuously learning new knowledge, skills, and methods can we become more capable of solving problems. In career development, we not only need to set clear goals for ourselves, but also develop plans and measures to achieve them. Only in this way can we plan our future life and work more clearly.

Understand one's personality and abilities

When choosing a career, we also need to understand our own personality and abilities. Only by working in the field we excel in can we become more proficient and do better. If we do not understand our own personality and abilities when choosing a profession, we may experience a situation of "going the other way". For example, you are an introverted person, but you are choosing a sales job. Sales work requires dealing with strangers, which requires you to have a certain level of interpersonal skills; Introverted people often lack the ability to interact with strangers. Therefore, when choosing a career, it is important to consider whether you have sufficient interpersonal skills. If we do not understand our own personality and abilities, we may affect our career development due to our lack of corresponding interpersonal skills. In addition, we also need to consider whether our interests and hobbies match our profession. Some people may be interested in a certain profession or industry, but that profession or industry may not be suitable for them. If we choose a job we don't like, we may not be able to do it well, let alone create a career. Only by finding a suitable job or profession can one become more proficient in pursuing it.

Looking at career development from a long-term perspective

Looking at career development from a long-term perspective will help you understand that all professions have their own lifecycle. During this cycle, it may change, but this change will not be too significant. If you can take advantage of this change as an opportunity, it can bring huge benefits to your career. If you are passionate about a certain industry or profession, then you should take advantage of it as an opportunity. Don't treat your career as a job. Because it will change over time. If you cannot treat your career like you do your job, then this job is not the one you like.

The rapid development of artificial intelligence (AI) has a huge impact on traditional industries and professions. For many people, this means there may be many new career choices in the future. We all know that from a technical perspective, AI is a promising new technology. It can help us create more new career opportunities. But how does AI work? How do you determine the most promising career path in an AI driven world? To some extent, this is the topic we are discussing here today: career choice. In terms of career choice, you need to consider many factors. You need to understand what your job or profession means for your personal and professional development, and what makes it more promising.

The biggest motivation for choosing a career is your interest in it. If you don't have genuine enthusiasm, you won't have the motivation to do a job you enjoy. If you feel uncomfortable with what you are doing, even if it is very promising, you may not have the motivation to do it. Therefore, when we consider careers, the first thing to consider is what interests us. This means checking whether the industry has enough opportunities for us to come into contact with it and make us feel excited. If you don't have enough motivation, you may not be able to gain a sense of achievement and satisfaction from it. In other words, if you are not interested in a certain profession or industry, even if it seems promising, it may not truly make you happy. For example, suppose you want to be a teacher, but you don't like this industry. That's why it's important to consider interests when choosing a career. In fact, this is one of the most important things we have been talking about. I have written an article before to discuss this topic: no matter what industry or job we are in, as long as we are truly interested and engaged in it, we will have the motivation to do it. Therefore, if we enjoy a job or profession, then go ahead and do it! When you enter a new industry, if you have enough motivation to pursue this job or profession, even if it seems promising, it doesn't matter. That's why I often encourage people to focus on what they enjoy early in their careers. This will help them find and persist. This is a very important thing when we consider the possibility of more new professions appearing in the future. There is no need to consider too many other factors.

When considering career choices, you need to understand whether the job or profession you are engaged in requires a specific skill set. For example, if you want to become an accountant, you need to have some financial knowledge and skills. This means understanding your interests, talents, abilities, and personality, and then considering how they combine to create a unique skill set. This can give you a greater sense of achievement and joy in your work.

These skill combinations include knowledge related to your interests and skills. For example, if you are good at communication and writing, then you may be more suitable for work related to this. If you are good at teamwork and leadership skills, you may play an important role in some jobs that require leadership skills. If you have a strong interest in organizational theory, business processes, time management, project management, etc., then you may become an excellent manager. If you are good at computer programming and software development, you may become a programmer or software engineer. If you are interested in business, finance, and human resources, you may work in related fields such as finance, human resources, and marketing. Only when we know what we are good at and what we are not good at, can we find truly meaningful things in our work.

Your interest and enthusiasm are the key factors that determine whether you enjoy this job. If you don't like the job you're doing, even with a lot of money, it can make you feel uncomfortable. This is also why some people can still achieve good results in careers they do not like. But if you are very interested in a certain job and willing to work hard for it, then there is a possibility of success. For example, if you enjoy photography or painting, you can consider becoming a professional photographer.

Experience is a crucial factor as it can help you determine your abilities and strengths. Without experience, you cannot achieve success. However, not all experiences will have the same impact on you. Experience can help you understand your own abilities and strengths, making it easier for you to adapt to new environments. This is a very important factor in your career. But there are also some exceptions. For example, if you have had a failed project, you may feel that you do not have the ability to succeed in a new project, so you will not be able to achieve success. In fact, although success is a factor, it is not the most important factor. In your career, experience can also help you better understand your abilities and strengths. For example, if you have worked in a sales related field before, going into sales now may be more helpful. But this does not mean that people without previous sales experience cannot do a good job in sales. As long as they have experience in communication skills, motivation, leadership, and time management skills, they have the potential to become successful salespeople. If you have a successful entrepreneurial experience, it will become easier when you start your own company. This is because various risks and opportunities need to be considered during the entrepreneurial process. In addition, if you have a management team or have led a team before, it will also be helpful to you. This may mean becoming a manager after working for a few years in a large company. This is particularly important for those who already have experience in one or more industries. They have already had a job or career experience, and they possess some skills and knowledge to help them achieve this goal. Therefore, experience can also help you determine the most promising career path.

Another important factor in choosing a job or profession is your skill level. It refers to your basic skills, such as communication, writing, problem solving, critical thinking and creativity. This is the way you communicate and establish relationships with others. A promising career will cultivate you into an efficient, successful, and adaptable person. If you find yourself unable to handle this job, then you are not prepared and will need some time to adjust. In fact, according to Fortune magazine, artificial intelligence will take millions of jobs in the coming decades. These job positions will cause many people to lose their jobs, which brings enormous pressure to many people. If you can increase your skill level for yourself or your profession, then you can achieve success in the workplace without worrying about losing your job. In addition, as the world shifts towards digitization and intelligence, many people's skill levels may decline. This means that they must maintain competitiveness by improving their skills. This is a good starting point before you learn how to increase your skill level for yourself or your profession.

Navigating the Job Market with AI

Is artificial intelligence going to improve the world? In a recent survey about potential careers, more than half of respondents asked this question. The following is their most frequently asked query: What would you like to do if you were AI? The term "artificial intelligence" is frequently associated with robotics or robotics technology. In point of fact, when we discuss AI, we are referring to computer programs. PC projects (or programming) have their own capacities, knowledge, and feelings, and can advance freely and consistently work on all the while. Now, we can also say that, to a certain extent, AI systems can already perform many tasks for humans. What does it imply? Do some individuals believe that AI will simplify our work? Or will it enhance our enjoyment of our profession?

On the surface, artificial intelligence appears to be a very advanced technology that can assist us in completing a variety of tasks at work. Notwithstanding, since these innovations were created from our human mind, it is hard to recognize whether they were developed by people or framed normally. Some people think that many human jobs will be replaced by artificial intelligence, while others think that it might create more jobs. As a result, I'd like to talk about this problem from our point of view. Will man-made reasoning altogether change our professions? The response is "yes." In the coming decades, many people believe that artificial intelligence will alter our careers. For the people who have worked in this field for a long time and will keep on working in it, this is uplifting news. In any case, for the people who are simply starting to embrace this arising field and need to work in it, this is certainly not something to be thankful for. There are many things that artificial intelligence can do, but some things will never be automated like machines. That is the reason many individuals accept that man-made consciousness will supplant numerous human positions in their professions. However, there are also some occupations that still require human labor, such as those in the financial services, legal, and healthcare sectors. By the by, certain individuals actually inquire, "Will computerized reasoning make us jobless?" The way to addressing this question is the way we view it. It's possible that the things we do do not live up to our expectations. In point of fact, even if artificial intelligence systems are aware of what humans are saying, it is difficult for them to comprehend what they are saying, so when AI systems say, "Please give me a cup of coffee," it is difficult for us to comprehend this sentence. So, what is the solution? The response to this question is, to a certain extent, " What if I can't do this? At the end of the day, when we ask ourselves "How would it be advisable for me I guarantee that I will not lose my employment," the response is: " To adapt to this new position, I need a skill. Despite the fact that AI will expand employment opportunities in numerous sectors (but not necessarily all professions), Be that as it may, now and again (like monetary administrations), this can likewise bring a few adverse consequences, (for example, robo computerized financial business). In a nutshell, many fields will benefit from increased employment opportunities and artificial intelligence; However, not all positions are available to everyone. Accordingly, don't be excessively hopeful that computer based intelligence will supplant many individuals' work positions.

WORK 2.0: HOW ARTIFICIAL INTELLIGENCE IS CHANGING THE FUTURE OF WORK

With the development of artificial intelligence, it has begun to participate in the labor market, albeit to a very limited extent. In essence, AI technology can assist us in reducing numerous repetitive tasks. For instance, "natural language processing" refers to the process by which large amounts of data are fed into a model so that it can learn how to make predictions. Regular language handling is an innovation that can change words and expressions in text into designs that can utilized for model. This indicates that artificial intelligence can function without human comprehension and explanation. On the basis of this, these technologies make it possible for machines to take the place of humans when it comes to performing tedious and repetitive tasks like file classification, processing financial data, and medical diagnosis. Artificial intelligence may even, in some instances, take the place of human workers without the involvement of legal or human resources departments. "Automation," for instance, is used to replace warehouse workers, couriers, and cashiers in countries like the United States and Canada. The computerization of these positions might prompt decreased pay or joblessness for certain individuals. Be that as it may, it might likewise set out new position open doors for other people. As we will see in the following section, AI can assist us in solving numerous issues and completing tasks more quickly. Furthermore, man-made intelligence can likewise assist us with better figuring out ourselves as well as other people. Involving man-made consciousness in the work environment implies that we will actually want to more readily comprehend ourselves as well as other people to settle on better choices in any circumstance. AI can help us make better choices and work together to solve problems. This assists with decreasing dynamic blunders and further develop effectiveness, without stalling out or confounded like people do. Man-made consciousness can assist us lay out great associations with partners and clients and further develop the workplace. It can also help us finish things faster and work more efficiently in some cases. Man-made brainpower can likewise set out new open doors for people to take care of already unsolvable issues, for example, populace maturing and natural harm. In fact, many professions deal with issues like conflict, resource scarcity, population pressure, and climate change. Basically, man-made reasoning empowers people to finish jobs that recently expected people to do and further develop efficiency, yet it might likewise prompt joblessness for specific laborers (like those participated in monotonous and drawn-out work) or face imbalance for specific people, (for example, those in places that require elevated degrees of expert information and abilities). In essence, this is why, in many instances, we need to think about these issues and look at our skills and abilities in order to figure out how AI can benefit our workplace. Artificial intelligence can also assist humans in coping with their own health issues and improving their own health status. Using artificial intelligence, for instance, in medicine can help doctors better serve their patients and cut down on the amount of time spent on diagnostic procedures. Artificial intelligence (AI) has the potential to assist humans in enhancing their own quality of life and working conditions (such as workplace automation). Artificial intelligence can also assist individuals in reducing medical and other costs and improving their own health in this circumstance.

Many people are under the impression that the development of artificial intelligence and automation systems will result in

WORK 2.0: HOW ARTIFICIAL INTELLIGENCE IS CHANGING THE FUTURE OF WORK

an increase in employment opportunities and, as a result, an increase in income. However, when we refer to robotics technology, we are actually referring to artificial intelligence. Presently, advanced mechanics innovation is turning out to be progressively normal in numerous ventures, from assembling to medical care and horticulture. There will be more job opportunities in these fields as technology continues to advance. In the long run, artificial intelligence technology has the potential to create not only new employment opportunities but also new revenue opportunities. I believe this transformation will be beneficial, despite the fact that it will take time. People will be able to take advantage of the environment's constant change as long as they are open to this new technology. For instance, individuals will be able to earn more money as new technologies are implemented and used in the workplace and industry.

In this article, we will explore how artificial intelligence and machine learning can help companies and job seekers create better job experiences. I have seen people say, 'Do you know? I studied computer science in college, but I didn't do well in math classes. What would you do?' This is a very typical problem because it reflects some of the problems faced by traditional university education. In fact, courses like computer science are often considered outdated because they can make you lose interest in what you are learning. However, in fact, computer science is a very useful discipline, especially for those who want to succeed in their work

How Artificial Intelligence Changes Our Way of Employment

To help you understand how artificial intelligence and machine learning have changed our way of employment, please imagine that this is a very busy job search process. During this process, employers hope to understand the skills and experience of candidates to help them determine what kind of employees they need and how to manage them. When you are looking for a job, employers can start with a platform: communicate with potential job seekers through online chat, social media, and other means. Once you have this information, you can contact the company via email, text message, or phone to obtain detailed information about your skills and experience. This is a typical process: job seekers contact their employers through online chat and social media, and they will receive emails, text messages, or phone calls. However, for some companies, this process may be too time-consuming or inefficient. To address this issue, employers can use artificial intelligence technology to manage their recruitment process. This can make the entire process more automated and enable faster completion of a series of tasks. For example, in a recent article published by Business Insider, we explored how machine learning can help employers create better recruitment processes. For many job seekers, this is a challenging task as they typically need to interact with multiple different companies to find a job that suits them.

Using Artificial Intelligence to Solve the Challenges of Traditional University Education

The rapid development of artificial intelligence (AI) and machine learning is changing educational institutions. You can use them to change your learning style and focus more on learning instead of sitting there playing games or doing boring things all day. In the past few years, great progress has been made in artificial intelligence and machine learning. It is helping educational institutions solve a key problem: how can these tools be used to help students achieve higher scores and better grades? I think there are many ways to do this. We have developed some tools that can help students improve their exam scores. For example, we have a Pearson Video Plan (PV) An application that can analyze students' performance in different exams. Then, we can help them improve their grades by adjusting our courses. This means that if you achieve good grades in the learning process, you should not be surprised because you know you can do it But another method is to use artificial intelligence and machine learning to check students' learning progress.

Machine learning can help job seekers prepare for work

In some cases, job seekers may need to make adjustments to their skills to help them stand out in the job market. For example, for those who want to work in the construction industry, they may need to learn more about how to use CAD and Sketch. For those who want to work in software development, this may mean they need more knowledge about programming languages, such as Python, C++, or Java. Equally important, machine learning can help job seekers understand areas they may not be familiar with, thereby better preparing their resumes and interviews. For example, if you want to become a software engineer or designer, you need to know how to create presentations, use software, use online tools such as Codecademy, and how to design and test applications. By learning machine learning techniques, you can better understand your skills and match them with the skills available in the current job market. For example, if you have a software development or design job, machine learning can help you understand how to create a simple project, how to handle large datasets, and how to create documents and charts. If you are interested in technology and business, machine learning can help you understand some industry trends, company strategies, and what kind of talent recruiters are looking for.

Provide artificial intelligence solutions for enterprises

One benefit of using artificial intelligence in recruitment is that it can help recruiters make better decisions for future employees. Imagine if you use machine learning technology in recruitment, you will be able to find your favorite job, "he said. If you can predict which candidates will join your team, it would be great. Artificial intelligence technology can be used to predict whether candidates are suitable for company culture. Artificial intelligence and machine learning technologies can help us understand whether people have the right feelings about their work and provide us with better methods to decide who should stay in the company. This will enable companies to better understand what kind of employees they need. Human intelligence can also help companies improve operational efficiency. Utilizing machine learning technology to track productivity and adjust based on real-time data will enable companies to make smarter decisions. This data-driven decision-making can help companies organize and manage their business more effectively, and help them invest funds in more efficient work, "he said.

Make your resume more personalized

Due to its ability to quickly and accurately understand your experience and the challenges you may face in the job search process, artificial intelligence can help you stand out from the competition. Of course, this does not mean that you should ignore skills in the job search process. On the contrary, you should strive to learn the skills required for each job. Additionally, if you are very interested in a particular skill, it is best to include it in your resume Reflected. You can add some specific descriptions to your resume to illustrate this point, or directly highlight skills related to the job When you have a clear vision of the career you want to pursue, you can write it on your resume and explain it as detailed as possible. However, this does not mean that you must tell the hiring manager all the details about the project and job description. On the contrary, it means that you should show them something they may not know how to complete. For example, if they know that a job requires programming language And machine learning algorithms, then this resume will be more suitable for them. But for those unfamiliar with technical languages and machine learning algorithms, this does not necessarily mean anything. It is important to focus on showing the interviewer that they are good at problem-solving, coding, teamwork, and problem-solving

Using AI to Improve Your Career

If you are a non math major student or want to improve your math skills, using machine learning techniques may be helpful. You can use algorithms to predict which companies your resume will be pushed to and how your ranking in search results will change. If you need to send your resume to a specific company or position, AI can play a very important role throughout the entire process. It can help you find some things you need to know during the interview, so that you can focus on the most important questions during the interview. If you want to send a recruitment application to the company, you should understand how artificial intelligence can help the company screen resumes. Using machine learning, you can create a unique resume for each position. By using these technologies, companies can understand what they want from potential candidates and what content they should include in their resumes. Using machine learning, you can create a very personalized recommendation list that tells the company what kind of talent they need to fill vacant positions. Due to the fact that artificial intelligence is changing various aspects of our society, it will have a profound impact on the future. Artificial intelligence is a new technology that will change the way we work, live, and communicate in the coming years.

Automated resume and cover letter

In the past decade, the use of automated resumes and cover letters has become the standard for corporate recruitment, and there has been significant progress in this process. Companies that use automated resumes and cover letters can use artificial intelligence technology to analyze thousands of resumes and cover letters, thereby better understanding the skills, work experience, and work motivation of job seekers. In the past, these analyses often took two to three weeks to complete. In 2019, IBM partnered with Amazon to help companies better screen resumes and provided 1 million automated resumes and cover letters within approximately two weeks. Google has recently started using artificial intelligence to automatically generate resumes. This technology was developed by Google's artificial intelligence team to help businesses quickly create a digital, automated resume and cover letter. Google uses machine learning and natural language processing to analyze resumes and automatically generate cover letters, making them faster and more accurate than traditional methods. According to a 2019 study by Harvard Business Review magazine, approximately 60% of recruiters stated that they typically use artificial intelligence to check job seekers' resumes and cover letters. Although this proportion may be higher, overall, over 70% of recruiters say they use artificial intelligence technology to screen resumes, write cover letters, and interview Q&A.

Screening resumes and interviews

Many people have had the experience of searching for many companies, positions, and job descriptions online, only to find that they don't know how to filter resumes. Therefore, many job seekers choose to seek help directly from the company. But with the continuous development of technology, many companies have begun to use artificial intelligence technology to screen resumes and provide suggestions based on the skills and experience of job seekers. This is beneficial for both employers and job seekers. For employers, this can make their search for talent faster and more effective, while also avoiding spending a lot of time in interviews because they do not need to personally screen resumes or conduct interviews. For job seekers, this can improve their work efficiency because they don't have to spend a lot of time and effort on resumes, just use artificial intelligence technology to screen out the most suitable job for them. RICS suggestion: If you are looking for a job that matches your skills and experience, then you should use artificial intelligence technology to filter your resume. If you are looking for a better job, you can use artificial intelligence technology to optimize your resume, screen suitable candidates, and design interview questions. This may be difficult for you, but when you start using artificial intelligence technology, you will find it a very efficient way to help you find a good job.

3. Assess work abilities and experience

AI can help employers understand employees' work experience, so as to make more intelligent decisions in recruitment and talent management. For example, a study by the Institute of Chartered Surveyors (CMI) in the UK found that 50% of artificial intelligence systems can predict whether candidates meet job requirements based on data-driven methods. However, if your employer wants to learn more about how you are doing at work, they may need to evaluate your skills and abilities through training and testing. That's why artificial intelligence can help companies identify potential talents and skills. For example, AI can assist the human resources department in evaluating candidates during the recruitment process, thereby providing more valuable insights for the company. Of course, companies need to ensure that the talents they choose are the most suitable, effective, and valuable. It is equally important to remember that no job is perfect - so don't worry about what you or your company will do in the next year. Instead, focus on cultivating talent for the future. When investing in recruitment and training, please ensure that you have a mature and effective structure to evaluate each candidate.

4. Predict which positions will be accepted

In the past, companies typically attempted to predict which positions would be hired, but with the help of technology, this process became easier. In a 2018 study, a startup called DeepWise used machine learning algorithms to predict which positions were likely to be hired and provided advice to businesses on how to utilize this information. Researchers have found that companies can use machine learning to predict which positions are most likely to be hired. For example, a startup called Ozon has developed a tool that can predict which positions will be hired. Our algorithm can analyze the connections between job applications and recruitment information. Then we will use machine learning algorithms to analyze whether these connections conform to what we call the 'correct' pattern, "said Jeremy Hands, CEO and co founder of the company.

5. Provide competitive wages and benefits

In recent years, employee welfare has become a hot topic. When artificial intelligence replaces humans, companies will have to start searching for those who can provide better benefits, but this may result in fewer job opportunities. Researchers are already using artificial intelligence to analyze people's work efficiency. They found that when employees are assigned to the same task, their working hours are shorter and they often repeat. They also found that artificial intelligence has an advantage in calculating the time required for a task compared to a traditional task. In addition, artificial intelligence can also help develop personalized welfare plans. For example, if an employee is assigned to a team for a research project, researchers can use artificial intelligence to predict the cost and time expenditure of the project, in order to provide better benefits. If enterprises need to pay more costs to support research projects, artificial intelligence can help them make wise decisions before they start. It can be said that artificial intelligence has brought a better and more competitive compensation strategy to companies. Although this will require time and technological change to achieve, it may be a trend in the coming years.

Are you ready in the era of artificial intelligence?

Finally, let's review some important facts about artificial intelligence: 1. Artificial intelligence can improve efficiency, but it cannot completely replace humans. Artificial intelligence is not the universal key to solving all problems. It can only solve existing problems and help us learn from mistakes. 3. The application of artificial intelligence in recruitment is rare. Compared to traditional recruitment methods, it is not good enough and requires more manpower and time. 4. Artificial intelligence cannot replace the unique advantages of human emotions, creativity, and interpersonal communication. Humans are often able to identify the emotions of others and make better decisions through their own intuition and behavior. We should cultivate creativity in new ways of working and understand how to judge our suitability through our intuition and behavior.

Thriving in an AI-Powered Workplace

With the rapid development of artificial intelligence and other advanced technologies, many companies are applying them to the workplace. Enterprises are now investing in more technology to support their employees and customers, and provide a better customer experience. In addition, these companies are looking for new ways to utilize their employees' time and establish better relationships with them. For employees, they usually consider artificial intelligence and other advanced technologies to be a burden in the workplace. However, when they truly use these technologies, they will find that they are not only tools for improving efficiency and productivity, but also can promote a better customer experience. Artificial intelligence and other advanced technologies can help businesses save a lot of time and provide a better customer experience. One of the biggest benefits for employees is that they can work from their own homes instead of going to the office. As companies can use these technologies to improve employee productivity and productivity, they are also able to work from home, providing employees with a new opportunity to establish relationships and work relationships. Most importantly, when we want to achieve these goals, we must first understand which technologies can help us achieve this. Artificial intelligence and other advanced technologies can improve productivity and productivity, but they may also increase workload and cause conflicts. Before starting to use these technologies, some preliminary investigation work must be carried out to ensure that they align with the company's values, culture, goals, and objectives. Here are some key considerations to pay attention to when using these technologies in the workplace:

Determine their goals

Enterprises should first determine their goals to ensure that they use artificial intelligence and other advanced technologies. The goals of enterprises should be directly related to the business outcomes they want to achieve. For example, if a company wants to improve customer satisfaction, they should understand to what extent they want employees to improve customer satisfaction. However, if companies only use artificial intelligence and other advanced technologies to improve customer experience, they will face enormous risks. The final outcome may disappoint the company as it is not based on specific business outcomes and goals, but rather on what employees believe is best. For example, if a company is striving to improve customer satisfaction and become a better team, then it needs to consider how to utilize artificial intelligence and other advanced technologies to achieve this goal. If a company wants to reduce employee dissatisfaction caused by excessive workload, it can consider using artificial intelligence and other advanced technologies to improve employee productivity and productivity. No matter what technology companies use to improve their business outcomes or customer experience, they need to determine how they can bring maximum value to the company. Once they have identified these goals, they can develop plans to achieve them.

Ensure that they understand the risks of using these technologies

WORK 2.0: HOW ARTIFICIAL INTELLIGENCE IS CHANGING THE FUTURE OF WORK

Although these technologies can improve our productivity, they also have potential risks. We should always keep this in mind and consider the risks involved before using these technologies. Due to the fact that artificial intelligence and other advanced technologies can help us do more, it may increase our workload. To ensure that everyone is aware of the risks that these technologies may bring, companies should conduct regular training to help employees understand the situations in which using these technologies may have a negative impact on them. After employees understand these risks, they can better collaborate with the company and conduct testing and improvement within the company. For example, an example where artificial intelligence systems may have a negative impact on employees is the use of robots for daily task processing. If robots are unable to perform or complete certain tasks, companies should consider whether adjustments need to be made among their employees. The same principle applies to artificial intelligence systems themselves. For example, if an artificial intelligence system is unable to predict what action the next user will take, or takes action when it should not, then the company should consider whether adjustments are needed. Another noteworthy issue is data security and privacy. For companies, ensuring data security and privacy before using these technologies is crucial. This can help employees stay focused and better manage their data. Furthermore, it is important to understand the situations in which the use of these technologies may have negative impacts. For example, if employees are informed that their personal information (including email, phone number, email address, financial information) will be recorded and tracked, they may feel uncomfortable and want to prevent the collection of this information.

Provide training and support

If companies do not understand the technology they are using, they will not be able to fully utilize these technologies. In addition, if the company does not provide training, they will find themselves facing bottlenecks in their work because they do not know how to handle these technologies. This means that when an employee uses these technologies in their work, they will feel confused and unable to unleash their best potential. In order to help employees use these technologies, companies should provide training for employees. This may include training courses, online resources, virtual reality, or on-site demonstrations. In addition, companies should ensure that employees are provided with clear and consistent explanations about these technologies. Without appropriate training and support, employees will find it difficult to understand the role, advantages, and disadvantages of the technology they are using. If they do not understand the role, advantages, and disadvantages of these technologies, they may feel misunderstood or forgotten. Furthermore, if they do not know how to use these technologies in their work, they may find it difficult to use them in their work. Therefore, when companies provide training to employees, they should ensure that they understand the role, advantages, and disadvantages of these technologies. This means that they should provide some documents or video courses to help employees understand and master these technologies. In addition, companies should ensure that they provide employees with tools and resources to help them use these technologies. However, for many employees, it is common for them to not know how to use these technologies or lack training. Therefore, when employees find themselves unable to use certain tools or understand certain operations, they often feel confused or disappointed. To address this issue, companies should start this work before providing training to employees.

Engage employees in it

It is important to involve employees in the company. This not only helps employees better understand how to use technology, but also helps them contribute to the company. In addition, involving employees can also help them understand the use of technology and motivate them to work better. If the company is not interested in technology, then they will not use these technologies and will not contribute to the company. Establish a culture within the company where everyone has a say in their work and encourages them to conduct deeper research on technology. Employees usually believe that the company should provide them with the best conditions, so they do not need to participate in these technologies. However, if you involve employees, they will feel that they have made a contribution to the company, and they will also learn something from the company. What are the best practices for using artificial intelligence and other advanced technologies in the workplace? If you want to use these technologies in the workplace, you must first understand their application scenarios and the potential benefits they may bring. You must determine which technologies you can use to improve productivity and efficiency without causing conflicts. Finally, you must involve employees and give them a voice in their work.

Pay attention to privacy

In addition, they can also make employees feel uneasy as they can perform many work tasks that may not require more supervision and management. To ensure that we do not overly rely on these technologies, we need to consider which technologies can help us achieve these goals and ensure that some preliminary investigation work is carried out before starting to use them. In addition, we also need to consider how to manage these technologies. We need to ensure that the company's values, culture, goals, and objectives are aligned with these technologies.

Artificial intelligence (AI) and other technologies have begun to be applied in the workplace. But this does not mean that employees have mastered all the knowledge of this technology, or that they should be afraid of certain aspects of these technologies. In fact, this is a misconception because many employees actually believe that they are still in a certain state of learning. If you want to use these technologies in the workplace, please make sure you understand how they work. If you do not understand how artificial intelligence and other technologies affect your daily work, some problems may arise during this process. Please remember that you will not use AI and other technologies without any training or insufficient training. Therefore, if you do not understand how AI and other technologies work, you cannot use them. Therefore, it is crucial to keep employees informed of the latest developments in their field from the beginning. Otherwise, you may find yourself in a difficult situation or struggling to solve the problem. Here are a few best practices related to the application of AI and other technologies in the workplace:

Develop a training plan

WORK 2.0: HOW ARTIFICIAL INTELLIGENCE IS CHANGING THE FUTURE OF WORK

A good training plan is the foundation for your understanding of AI and other technologies before implementing them. If you do not understand how technology will change the workplace, then you cannot provide training for employees. If you think you know nothing about this, it's your own mistake. Firstly, determine what new technologies do you want employees to master? If you're not sure, then think about how to make them learn them. Learning more about how to apply AI and other technologies to the workplace can help you develop a plan and provide training when needed. When employees know that their field is undergoing changes, they will feel uncomfortable and will not feel that they have mastered certain technologies. Therefore, if you can educate employees about the latest technologies and provide them with the necessary training, you can reduce the uncertainty faced by employees in the workplace. For example, if you are developing a new product or service, an appropriate training may help reduce employees' fear and concern about the product or service. In this situation, providing training to employees from the very beginning is crucial. So what is appropriate training? Please remember that training should be targeted at everyone. No matter which technology you use, you should start from the most basic: (1) Understand the working principle, usage methods, and how to maintain the technology. If you are unfamiliar with certain new technologies or worried about not being able to master them, it is best not to start trying them. (2) Show employees some of the artificial intelligence and other technologies they can use and how to integrate them with their daily work. For example, if they don't know how to apply speech recognition to certain tasks in the workplace, they may not know how to use it to communicate with customers. (3) Training must be relevant to business needs. If you want to apply artificial intelligence and other technologies in this field to improve efficiency and reduce error rates, you must understand how artificial intelligence and other technologies change processes, automation levels in the workplace, and how to utilize this technology to improve efficiency. (4) Provide training before starting to use AI and other technologies. If you do not receive training during the initial use of this technology, it is impossible to avoid problems or may lead to their occurrence. For example, if you want to use machine learning in the workplace and improve efficiency, but do not have relevant training or experience to guide you on what problems or situations may arise when using this technology. (5) If training is required for employees, please consider linking the training content to the latest industry standards and best practices. For example, if you want to understand how to handle unexpected situations and related issues when using applications in the workplace, what will happen or how these issues will be resolved.

Encourage employees to participate in online courses

If you want to keep employees informed of the latest developments in their field, you must first make them aware of the latest technologies. To ensure that this knowledge is disseminated within the organization, please try providing some guidance through online courses or videos. For example, you can provide employees with guidance on how to create accessibility and consistency, which can be found on a training platform. You can also provide employees with suggestions on how to improve existing processes. To ensure that employees are aware of the latest technological developments, please involve them in online courses and learn how to use new technologies. For example, if you want to use AI and other technologies for automation or predictive maintenance, you must let employees know how to use this technology. However, if you are unable to provide these contents to employees, it may cause them to feel confused or misled. Therefore, please involve employees in online courses or videos to help them understand the latest technological developments. This may make employees feel frustrated or difficult to answer their questions. However, if they feel confused, they will seek solutions or suggestions within the organization. As these issues cannot be resolved within the company, it is best to communicate them to others within the organization to address them.

Setting Milestones

You should also let employees understand how the technology they use will affect their daily work. This means letting them know, for example, that new technologies may have an impact on their work in terms of employee health and safety. If you are conducting training on new technologies, you must let employees know how the technology affects their daily work. You can view it as educating employees so that they can use these technologies in their daily work. In any case, before implementing new technologies, employees must be made aware of how these technologies will affect their daily work. You can provide employees with training on how to use AI and other technologies, or you can provide them with education on how using new technologies may affect their daily work. By discussing with employees at the beginning how the technology will affect their work, employees can understand how the new technology they are using affects their daily work. This will keep employees curious and enthusiastic about AI and other technologies. This can be achieved by providing training to employees on the impact of new technologies on their daily work. For example, if you are conducting training on how AI and other technologies affect their daily work, you can initially provide training to employees on how AI and other technologies will affect your daily work. Provide training to employees at the beginning on how new technologies will affect your daily work, which can keep them curious and enthusiastic about AI and other new technologies.

Use intelligent tools to track progress

Although AI and other technologies are advanced, you still need to train them. Some employees may be unfamiliar with AI and other technologies, so if you want them to know how to use AI and other technologies, you need to make them understand their functions and working principles. If you want to track certain progress, you need to use intelligent tools to track them. For example, if you want to track automated operations or budget expenditures, you can use these tools. Therefore, you can train employees to understand the working principles of AI and other technologies and understand their applications. This will make it easier for them to use these technologies to complete tasks.

Teams can follow a few best practices when working with AI and other advanced technologies in the workplace. To ensure that man-made insight advancements are meeting their primary objective and upgrading the business, they should at first recognize use cases and change existing data. To show the way that innovation can help the association, resourcing effect ought to likewise be thought about while exhibiting the mission.

WORK 2.0: HOW ARTIFICIAL INTELLIGENCE IS CHANGING THE FUTURE OF WORK

A solid understanding of software engineering and AI development is necessary for the facilitation of sophisticated automated analytics and the creation of adaptive AI systems. Artificial intelligence can be provided to employees by businesses as a tool for better decision-making and advanced insight. But it's important to remember that AI shouldn't completely replace human decision-making; rather, it should make it better. Calculations ought to be prepared as per the latest artificial intelligence and other high level work environment advances as a team with business partners. Additionally, prescriptive examination can be used to naturally decide.

In order to increase the likelihood of simulated intelligence being used in the workplace, it is essential to investigate cutting-edge methods like automating repetitive tasks and utilizing generative artificial intelligence to improve development efficiency. Work that uses computer-based intelligence can also benefit from hiring telecommuters. To settle on better choices for your association, it is crucial for stay aware of the latest advancements in your field. Prescriptive analytics can also be used to make decisions automatically.

To work on new innovation and increment representative productivity, adjusting representatives and laborers to the latest headways in your industry is fundamental. Even though cutting-edge innovations like computer-based intelligence can help you grow your business, it's important to use the right strategies.

Even though AI and other cutting-edge technologies can help you grow your business, it's important to use the right strategies. One of the most amazing practices is keeping up with innovations and learning development trends. Utilizing the most recent technologies, joining online communities, watching instructional videos, and attending conferences are all examples of this. It's important to have skills that are relevant to your industry and easy to find online.

In today's fast-paced workplace, staying up to date on the latest mechanical developments is essential. Chatbot development may actually be one of the most important mechanical advancements. In order to work effectively with simulated intelligence and other cutting-edge innovations in the workplace, it is essential to keep your knowledge base current through a variety of sources, such as online classes and web-based courses. Employees can also learn how to use new technology effectively by participating in video meetings that provide crucial information metrics. In a similar vein, managers ought to collaborate with their employees in order to facilitate requests and communicate the advantages of brand-new, automated frameworks. One should focus on mechanical progression and watch out for important information sources to turn into a fruitful quick supporter.

To get the best results from AI models and other cutting-edge technologies used in the workplace, it's important to follow best practices. For instance, if you use artificial intelligence to create sales messages or make smart choices, you should keep up with the most recent developments in your field.

It is essential to educate your AI model and provide it with reliable data sets in order to work effectively with AI and other advanced technologies in the workplace. This integrates setting up your model and organizing it as shown by your business targets. To really convey your computerized reasoning model, you should incorporate specialists and man-created knowledge specialists who can help you in making informed figures and tracking down plans in your data. In addition, in order to ensure that you will always receive accurate results, it is essential to continuously enhance your data set.

A comprehensive data strategy must be developed in order to work effectively with AI and other advanced technologies in the workplace. This remembers putting for place a learning the board framework as well as unambiguous procedures for naming information administration, accessibility information marking, and preparing. It is essential to make certain that your data can be evaluated in regulated resources and that advancement is used for availability getting. It is essential to comprehend districts where devices can be used to pool data from diverse structures and screen HR-related information in order to stay up to date on the most recent developments in your field.

While working with artificial intelligence and other state of the art advancements in the work environment, there are a couple of best practices to remember. Understanding the full range of AI capabilities and how they can be applied to specific pipelines or workflows is crucial. Using data examination to inspect industry data and further foster your capacities is one strategy for accomplishing this. In addition, educating your group on the most efficient methods for utilizing reproduced information and new capabilities can expedite their use. It is essential to act as a mentor or advisor to other people and to remain informed about the current trends in the job market in order to remain current on the most recent developments in your field.

While working with man-made intelligence and other trend setting innovations in the work environment, exploring different computer based intelligence technologies is fundamental. You can select the technology platforms that best utilize artificial intelligence for your business by utilizing your knowledge of the various platforms. Flexibility should be taken into consideration by both simulated intelligence analysts and those who use artificial intelligence innovations. You can locate potential applicants who have investigated thousands, if not millions, of controlled data of interest by utilizing social profiles. Flexibility and adaptability are essential for ensuring optimistic hopes for the future.

Workplaces are increasingly adopting cutting-edge technologies like AI. Because these technologies have the potential to have a significant impact on society, it is essential to use ethical judgment and adhere to ethical standards when working with them. In order to make well-informed decisions, people need to stay up to date on the most recent developments in their field. One way to do this is to keep up with workplace technologies, standards, and practical methods by going to conferences or webinars.

In order to transform our society into one that is driven by information, we must embrace simplicity and independence. Establishing straightforwardness systems, such as the distribution of results and autonomous reviews, can assist in fostering trust in mechanized decisions made by simulated intelligence. You can also guarantee that decisions are made with the best intentions if your business has empowered employees who are familiar with the AI source code. Participating in gatherings, taking online courses, and adhering to free rules are essential for staying up to date on the most recent developments in your field.

Ethical Considerations in an AI World

The rise of AI technologies has led to new AI technologies that have the potential to revolutionize the workplace and society. However, these advances also raise ethical issues that need to be addressed. The impact of the moral hazard associated with AI systems falls on workers, employers, and society as a whole. Therefore, technology developers in the field of technology should take into account social and ethical responsibilities. The misuse or potential negative impact of AI can have serious consequences for society. Conversely, embracing AI can also improve the workplace and make our lives better.

With the rise of HR technology, the use of AI in the recruitment process is becoming more and more common. However, while AI can help employers recruit talent more efficiently, it can also have an ethical impact on workers and society as a whole. One concern is that AI may automate tasks previously done by humans, reducing the overall meaning of work. This can lead to job losses and implicate employees who may not have the skills needed to adapt to their new roles. Ethical considerations also arise when considering how AI can limit human autonomy in the decision-making process. In addition, technology companies must consider the injustices and harms that their products may cause and strive to provide technology that meets the principles of fairness and justice. Business leaders should also be mindful of these ethical implications when implementing AI in the workplace. They should prioritize training opportunities for employees whose roles may be affected by automation, and have policies in place to protect employee rights. Conversely, embracing AI can also improve the workplace and make our lives better.

The increased use of AI in the workplace has ethical implications for workers, employers, and society as a whole. Overseeing AI deployment and managing machine work is critical to freeing human employees from repetitive tasks and allowing them to focus on more useful tasks that require human interaction. However, this requires personnel training and supervision to ensure worker safety. In warehouses, robots can increase workload, but also increase workers' chances of taking on higher-paying positions that require more complex skills. However, this also increases the risk for employees, who may face unemployment or displacement in some cases.

The increasing use of AI in the workplace has a significant impact on workers, employers, and society as a whole. The shortage of automation and technology makes the use of AI an attractive solution for companies looking to reduce labor costs. However, this also increases the risk for employees, who may face unemployment or displacement in some cases. The human workforce has skill capabilities that machines cannot replicate, and a significant reduction in the number of employees could mean that a company's skill capabilities will be reduced to a minimum.

The rise of artificial intelligence has forced organizations to establish working relationships with technology, introducing new ways of functioning the workforce. As technology provides alternative labor, the ethical challenges that come with it need to be addressed. The responsibility for using new technologies is to address ethical issues and ensure that people and technology can be integrated within the organization. Job portfolios now need to address ethical issues in organizational management because they bring people, workers and machines together. Integrating humans and machines into teams is the way forward, but it must be ethical to ensure a fair balance between human workers and technology.

It is essential to ensure that artificial intelligence is utilized in a responsible and ethical manner in light of the technology's ongoing development. The most vital move towards accomplishing this objective is to foster a moral structure for man-made consciousness to direct the turn of events and organization of computerized reasoning frameworks. Principles and normative statements of moral law, norms, and values ought to serve as the foundation for this framework. To ensure that trustworthy AI systems that do not infringe on the rights or privacy of individuals are developed, organizations must adhere to these ethical frameworks and the design principles of AI developers. In addition, a set of principles that will have a significant impact on our lives should serve as the foundation for the creation and application of artificial intelligence systems across all sectors.

It is essential to provide an ethical framework and guidelines for artificial intelligence in order to guarantee its responsible and ethical use. Responsible AI practices, such as ethical data governance, should be given priority when designing AI systems, and AI and AI ethics issues should be addressed. Ethical principles for making ethical decisions when designing and deploying artificial intelligence systems must be included in an effective governance framework. Establishing trust in governance within the industry is essential to ensuring that organizations are held accountable for their actions. Tending to explicit difficulties looked by associations, for example, decency and straightforwardness, will assist with utilizing these frameworks all the more dependably.

Man-made brainpower can possibly fundamentally alter our lifestyle and work. In any case, this innovation additionally brings moral situations that should be addressed to guarantee its dependable use. In order to accomplish this, businesses must incorporate AI ethics and ethical AI practices into the product development process. Continuously training AI models with various datasets that take fairness, bias, and interpretability into account is one approach. considering that these methods of theme building can boost trust in the products they use and increase efficiency. Also, associations ought to consider variety while creating man-made reasoning calculations and guarantee that information security is constantly safeguarded.

A human-driven approach to AI management should be adopted by businesses to ensure that computer-based intelligence is utilized consistently and ethically. All decision-making processes must prioritize ethical AI, and organizational bias must be reduced. Understanding your employees' needs, concerns, and expectations regarding AI technology and empathizing with them is essential. In a similar vein, businesses ought to make certain that day-to-day plans adhere to a security-first approach and place an emphasis on the protection of representatives throughout the working day. You will acquire a superior comprehension of how to utilize computerized reasoning artificially across an association, considering the necessities, everything being equal, in addition to the organization, by making a moral structure for simulated intelligence. In order to accomplish this, design controls must be implemented to ensure that all employees are consistently informed and that there are no mistakes made when using new technologies.

To ensure that AI is used in an ethical and responsible manner, it is essential to establish an ethical framework. The framework ought to include ethical guidelines for the use, analysis, and collection of data. Additionally, having an auditable technical framework will ensure that all AI systems are accountable and transparent. Knowing about the Ethics Committee will also help avoid any potential problems. As a component of the most common way of buying new innovations, it ought to be important to bring issues to light inside an association about moral computer based intelligence rehearses.

Conclusion: Embracing the Future of Work

Artificial intelligence and machine learning are rapidly ushering in a new era and reshaping our work processes. The way we behave both inside and outside of the workplace is being influenced by man-made consciousness, opening the door for rapid shifts in occupation markets and businesses.

From complex algorithms to natural language processing, AI technologies are rapidly entering numerous fields and industries with impressive results. Artificial intelligence is being utilized to robotize creation lines in manufacturing plants, to analyze and treat diseases in medical services, and to stop fake exchanges in banking. Data analysis, customer service, marketing, and even legal services are among the more complex applications of AI, and its scope is rapidly expanding beyond manual labor and industrial production.

Artificial intelligence is altering plans of action by providing arrangements that are more productive and financially savvy in addition to smoothing out everyday tasks. In a fraction of the time required by individuals, organizations can manage a large amount of information and direct intricate investigations. For instance, AI-powered software can go through legal documents and make better predictions about how cases will turn out. With simulated intelligence fueled chatbots now ready to overview clients on their inclinations and propose items with more noteworthy exactness than human client assistance specialists, artificial intelligence driven computerization can likewise lessen the time it takes to distinguish expected clients.

As AI continues to advance, so does its potential to alter employment markets. Representatives need to be able to adapt to the use of these innovations as simulated intelligence becomes increasingly adept at completing tasks that were previously completed by humans. Numerous new occupations and careers will emerge to accommodate those who wish to become proficient in AI-driven applications.

AI is altering our work practices and has numerous potential applications. Other than the way that PC based knowledge streamlining is how we finish things inside and outside the work space, yet it is similarly changing position advertises all around the planet. The use of artificial intelligence is expected to transform businesses and job descriptions in the near future.

As Artificial Intelligence (AI) technology develops, more people are questioning its implications in our lives. Despite its potential to automate mundane tasks and improve efficiency, AI cannot completely replace human intelligence and creativity.

AI is powered by algorithms. These algorithms are based on instructions given by a programmer, and can't use abstract or creative thought. AI lacks the capacity for problem solving and decision making like a human does- AI can identify a problem and respond with the exact programmed response. AI's lack of creativity means it can't come up with original ideas, or adapt to a changing environment.

In addition, AI can only operate within the parameters defined by its programmed instructions. It lacks the function of "thinking out of the box" that humans already possess. Human intelligence and creativity is about making connections, whereas AI is designed to interpret certain predetermined scenarios to deliver a specific result.

WORK 2.0: HOW ARTIFICIAL INTELLIGENCE IS CHANGING THE FUTURE OF WORK

Humans can also detect and respond to changes in surroundings and environment that AI cannot. We can differentiate between similar stimuli and interpret complex circumstances in ways AI cannot. For instance, if a machine-driven truck is set to make a delivery, it may be able to evaluate the sensory environment while driving, but it cannot understand the context of the situation or perceive possible irregularities, such as a faulty stop sign, the way a human driver can.

AI can certainly be beneficial in certain settings and circumstances. It can be used to automate processes and increase productivity, or provide data-driven decision-making. But it cannot replace the intelligence and creativity of a human, no matter how advanced the machine. AI can make our lives easier and more efficient, but it should always be viewed as a tool, and not an entire solution.

In the age of Artificial Intelligence (AI), staying ahead of the game has become increasingly important. AI, machine learning, and other technologies are rapidly advancing and transforming the way we live and work. As such, it is essential for workers to take a proactive approach to their own learning and continue to develop their skills in order to remain competitive in the job market. Through lifelong learning and continuous skill development, individuals can future-proof their careers and gain a critical edge in the rapidly changing world of AI and automation.

Lifelong learning is important as it allows individuals to stay up to date with changes and technology, as well as maintain a level of knowledge in their chosen profession. In a world where AI innovation is accelerating and automation is being used in many industries, having the most relevant skills that are in demand is of utmost importance. By taking courses and engaging in self-study, individuals can keep their knowledge current and acquire new skills which will help them stay ahead of the curve.

Continuous skill development is also important in the age of AI. As technology advances, jobs roles and their responsibilities evolve. By developing and honing your skills, you stay current on the latest advancements, become familiar with new technologies, and maintain your competitive edge. It also allows workers to adapt to the ever-changing needs of their industry as well as navigate any changes in their job role.

In the age of AI, lifelong learning and continuous skill development are essential in order to maintain competency and remain competitive in the job market. By keeping current on the latest technology, understanding the transformations that impact their industry and actively developing their skills, workers can ensure a secure career pathway and stay ahead of the curve.

The rise of artificial intelligence (AI) has shook up the job market in recent years. Many human jobs are being replaced by AI as robotics and other automated machines become more effective and accurate. This shift has significant ramifications for human work, and it highlights the significance of long lasting mastering and persistent expertise advancement.

Workers must constantly update and enhance their knowledge and skills in order to remain competitive in today's job market. The times of depending on one range of abilities to find a new line of work and give stable job are finished. In the period of simulated intelligence, laborers need to ceaselessly redesign and refresh their abilities to stay serious.

WORK 2.0: HOW ARTIFICIAL INTELLIGENCE IS CHANGING THE FUTURE OF WORK

In addition to assisting individuals in maintaining conversational relevance, continuous learning also aids in the development of confidence and resilience. Although AI can perform many tasks, it cannot yet replace human ingenuity and creativity. Workers must continuously update their skills in order to remain marketable and valuable.

People ought to likewise track down ways of using computer based intelligence innovation as a learning device. By exploring different avenues regarding simulated intelligence, laborers can rapidly level up their abilities and gain significant information and experience to acquire an edge in the gig market.

In addition, employers should encourage and support lifelong learning. This is already being done by a lot of businesses by providing mentorship opportunities, free online education resources, and other tools to help students learn.

To remain competitive in the job market in the age of AI, lifelong learning and continuous skill development are essential. Workers can harness the power of AI and acquire new and valuable skills that will enable them to advance in their careers if they adopt the right mindset and have access to the appropriate tools and resources.

The age of AI (artificial intelligence) has arrived. Learning new skills and staying up to date on technological advancements are essential for individuals to remain competitive in the job market as AI rapidly evolves and reshapes the way we think, work, and interact. Embracing lifelong learning and continuous skill development is necessary for this.

The market value of static knowledge systems is rapidly declining in the "new normal" of rapid technological advancement, and businesses are looking for people who are always willing to learn new skills. Not only is AI-powered technology altering the way we work, but it is also redefining the skills that employers seek in employees. The capacity of AI to automate routine tasks is a significant advantage. As a result, employees must possess highly sought-after abilities such as problem-solving, collaboration, creative thinking, and problem-solving skills.

Employees are equipped with the desired information and potential capabilities they need to actually implement initiatives and complete tasks with confidence thanks to lifelong learning and continuous skill development. This keeps them abreast of the expanding role that AI plays in the workplace. In addition, employees' value is raised and job satisfaction is enhanced by ongoing learning and skill development. Workers are happier and have a stronger sense of purpose in their roles when they can put their advanced skills to use.

The world is evolving quickly, and it's fundamental for laborers to remain on the ball. AI provides students with unprecedented opportunities to learn the skills necessary for each job role and remain up to date on the most recent technologies. Employees must be willing to embrace novel and potentially challenging work practices and prioritize skill development.

In the age of AI, businesses must ensure that their employees are up to date on the most recent technological developments and strive to cultivate a culture of continuous learning and development. They will be able to guarantee that their workers will continue to be competitive and reach their full potential by doing this.

- End -

Don't miss out!

Visit the website below and you can sign up to receive emails whenever Warren H. Lau publishes a new book. There's no charge and no obligation.

https://books2read.com/r/B-A-OZQW-PCGIC

BOOKS 2 READ

Connecting independent readers to independent writers.

Did you love *Work 2.0: How Artificial Intelligence is Changing the Future of Work*? Then you should read *Your System's Sweetspots: CEO's Advice on Basic Cyber Security*[1] by Warren H. Lau!

Computer Systems Nowadays have become more sophisticated, more convenient to use, however, the convenience comes in a price. The system nowadays are more vulnerable to cyber attacks!

What to do if your computer/ smartphone/ website server is compromised?

What to do if your email account is PWNed?

---

1. https://books2read.com/u/3nDRwK

2. https://books2read.com/u/3nDRwK

Or, if your friends, relatives or employers face the above problem, what would you do to help them?

In this book, you will learn about the most recent hackers tricks, most prevalent form of cyberattacks that personal computers and website managers nowadays have to deal with.

About the Author

Warren H. Lau is currently C.E.O. of a tech firm, and has many years of experience in overseeing web-based development projects.

The main duty of his job is to design and oversee the development of usable websites, mobile sites and mobile apps that are user friendly and immune to cyberattacks; at the same time, lead the marketing team to achieve business success.

Before Warren H. Lau begins his career in the technology industry, he spent more than ten years in the investment career, and succeeded through a combined application of fundamental, technical and news analysis. He summarized all his knowledge and experience and published his investment book series: "Winning Strategies of Professional Investment".

About the Publisher

INPress International is a global publication organization that focuses on knowledges and topics where the traditional schooling system do not provide. Our Mission is to build a more humanistic, fair and peaceful future through our publication works.